Contents

Introduction		2
Harvest	Christianity	3 – 6
Eid ul-Fitr	Islam	7 – 10
Yom Kippur and Sukkot	Judaism	11 – 14
Diwali	Sikhism	15 – 18
Guru Nanak's Birthday	Sikhism	19 – 22
Hanukkah	Judaism	23 – 26
Christmas	Christianity	27 – 30
Chinese New Year	Chinese Culture	31 – 34
Holi	Hinduism	35 – 38
Pesach	Judaism	39 – 42
Easter	Christianity	43 – 46
Baisakhi	Sikhism	47 – 50
Some Japanese and Chinese Festivals	Japanese and Chinese Culture	51 – 54
Wesak	Buddhism	55 – 58

Resource Sheet A
An overview of the cycle of festivals each year — 59

Resource Sheet B
An overview of the cycle of festivals each year continued — 60

Resource Sheet C
Religious symbols: Sikhism, Islam, Hinduism — 61

Resource Sheet D
Religious symbols: Buddhism, Christianity, Judaism — 62

Resource Sheet E
Festivals word puzzle — 63

Resource Sheet F
Festivals crossword — 64

Andrew Brodie: Festivals Across the Year 9-11 © A C Black Publishers Ltd. 2007

Introduction

This book features information and activity sheets on fourteen significant festivals throughout the year. It is designed to familiarise primary-aged children with some of the celebrations and customs of the world's major religions and cultures.

The festivals are arranged in approximate chronological order, starting from September and working across the school year. Note, however, that some festivals change date each year – the Christian festival of Easter and the Islamic festival of Eid ul-Fitr, for example. Further guidance about the order in which the festivals occur can be found on Resource Sheets A and B (page 59-60).

For each festival there are four pages, the first of which provides comprehensive background information for teachers followed by three worksheets. The worksheets are intended primarily for use in RE lessons but many could also be used in assemblies or in after school clubs. The sheets can be photocopied on to OHP transparencies and displayed for all to see. The worksheets should give children a good understanding of the story behind each religious or cultural festival, and some of the main traditions and customs involved.

At the end of the book there are six Resource Sheets for teachers. These sheets can be used to consolidate or expand the children's knowledge of the religions included in this book. These Resource Sheets include the following:

Resource Sheet A An overview of the cycle of festivals: Sikh, Islamic and Jewish

Resource Sheet B An overview of the cycle of festivals: Hindu, Christian, Buddhist and Chinese.

Resource Sheet C Religious symbols: Sikh, Islamic, Hindu.

Resource Sheet D Religious symbols: Buddhist, Christian, Jewish.

Resource Sheet E A festivals word puzzle. This puzzle is a consolidation and revision activity.

Resource Sheet F A festivals crossword, to help consolidate children's knowledge of festival names.

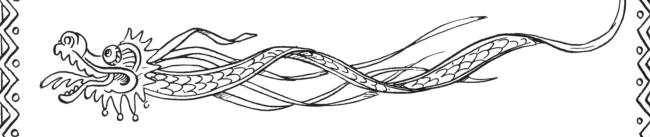

Harvest

Teacher's Notes

Background information

Harvest celebrations in Great Britain date back to long before the advent of Christianity. For as long as people have grown crops to eat, their survival has depended on the success of the harvest. Harvest festivals are believed to have become part of the Christian calendar in 1843 when a church in Cornwall held a special harvest thanksgiving service in the autumn of that year.

Christian churches now hold services with Harvest hymns and prayers each autumn, and are decorated with seasonal fruit and vegetables. This Harvest produce is often distributed to the elderly or those in need when the celebrations are over.

Now that so much of our food comes pre-washed, pre-chopped and pre-packaged from supermarkets, many children are so far removed from farming and food in its natural state that it is easy to forget the importance of a good harvest. Harvest festival provides a good opportunity to think about where foods come from and how and where they are grown. It can also provide an opportunity to discuss the contrast in food distribution between rich and poor countries, helping those in need, and being thankful for what we have.

Practical activities

Provide a variety of freshly grown produce for the children to look at and taste. Explain to pupils that not all items purchased from supermarkets are grown locally, and that many have had to be shipped thousands of miles from all around the world. Encourage pupils to recognise which items are fruit and which are vegetables, and to learn that fruit and vegetables are very important components in a healthy diet. Teach them that bread is made from wheat grown in the fields, and how a good or bad harvest affects all the food we eat.

Give the pupils simple pictures of plates on which to draw their favourite meals, and ask them to include both fruit and vegetable items. Alternatively, buy large and small paper plates for every member of the class on which to draw their healthy main course and healthy dessert.

Worksheet 1 Pupils will use their knowledge and skill to complete a Harvest information sheet. The missing words in the correct order are – Christians, autumn, fresh, trees, churches, wheat, crusty, plums, eating, bananas, carrots, fish, God, services, elderly, future. This sheet could be photocopied on to an OHP transparency and used as a focus activity in assembly.

Worksheet 2 A word puzzle.

Worksheet 3 Pupils are asked to take the words found in the puzzle on Worksheet 2 and sort them into categories.

Andrew Brodie: Festivals Across the Year 9-11 © A C Black Publishers Ltd 2007

3

Harvest

Name .... Date ....

Read the text below and fill in the spaces with words from the loaf.

services   autumn   Christians
trees   churches   fresh
plums   crusty   wheat   fish
carrots   future   bananas
elderly   God   eating

At Harvest time _____ give thanks to God for the food he has provided. In the UK, this is celebrated in early _____, as this is the time when many crops have been harvested from the fields, _____ vegetables are ready to eat and fruits on _____ are ripe. Many Christian _____ and schools will have large displays of food as part of their Harvest Festival celebrations.

The crops in the Harvest celebration might include _____, oats, barley and corn for breads and cereals. As part of a Harvest display you might also see freshly made loaves of _____ bread.

The fresh fruits that are often seen on Harvest displays are apples, pears and _____, as these are ready for _____ at this time of the year. However, now that many foods are transported from other parts of the world, it is not unusual to see pineapples, _____, oranges and many other different fruits.

You will find vegetables in most Harvest displays too, including onions, potatoes, _____ and cucumbers. Some Harvest celebrations also include food that comes from the sea, such as _____, lobster and crab.

As well as being a time for giving thanks to _____, it is a time to think about the needs of others. After Harvest _____ are held in churches, the food that has been used to decorate the buildings is distributed to the less fortunate people in the community. This might include the _____ or the poor. Modern Harvest festivals can also be a time to consider how the human race should protect the planet for _____ generations.

Harvest

Name .... Date ....

The puzzle below contains words that all have a connection to the Christian celebration of Harvest. To find out what the words are you must work out what letter is represented by each number. To start you off some of the letters have been provided. As you find each new letter enter it into the grid at the bottom of the page, and cross it off the list down the side of the page.

1	2	3	4	5	1	1	7	4			1	7	8	9
12					4				13					5
14				5		16		5		17	4	5	3	
5			17			8		23					18	
14		7		5		16		2					12	
12	3	2	12	3		9	8	25	25	4	7			
		9		5		9		20						
13	19	4		3		17			16	12	23			
		9	5	2	10	4		13				5		
		4		13		5				1				
6	20	4	7	26		16		7	12	17	25	14	4	13
20			12		12							2		
4			3		12	13	5	3	18	4			16	
5					3							12		
14	12	9	5	14	12		17	4	4	14	13	12	12	14

A
B
C
D
E̶
F̶
G
H
I̶
J
K
L
M
N̶
O
P̶
Q̶
R
S
T
U
V̶
W
X̶
Y
Z

1	2	3	4	5	6	7	8	9	10	11	12	13
P	I	N	E							X		

14	15	16	17	18	19	20	21	22	23	24	25	26
	Q						V	F		J		

Andrew Brodie: Festivals Across the Year 9–11 © A C Black Publishers Ltd 2007

Harvest

Name .... Date ....

Write the words you found on Worksheet 2 into the correct boxes on this page.

Seafood

Cereals

Fruit

Vegetables

Now see if you can add to each of the lists. Perhaps you can even complete each set of ten. You may need to use a dictionary to make sure you spell your new words correctly.

Eid ul-Fitr

Teacher's Notes

Background information

The Islamic faith is based on five ideals and beliefs called the Five Pillars of Islam. These are:

Shahadah – The Muslim profession of faith that there is only one God and Muhammad was His final prophet

Salah – Performing ritual prayers five times a day

Zakah – Giving a portion of one's wealth each year for charitable causes

Sawm – Fasting during the month of Ramadan

Hajj – Making a pilgrimage to the holy Ka'bah at Mecca.

Eid ul-Fitr (or Id ul-Fitr) is the festival which celebrates the end of the month of Ramadan, when Muslims fast every day from dawn until dusk. The fasting helps Muslims to remember when the prophet Muhammad was given the sacred texts which form the Qur'an, the holy book of Islam. It encourages self-discipline and also helps Muslims to understand the sufferings of the poor and hungry, and to have sympathy for them. During Ramadan there is a focus on prayer, reading and learning the Qur'an, forgiveness and charity. Muslims are discouraged from partaking in worldly pursuits such as idle chatter or watching television, and are expected to avoid any kind of evil thoughts or actions. Each day, after the sun has set, many people attend the mosque to eat together. Some people are excused from fasting at Ramadan, including those who are sick or very old, children under the age of twelve, and those travelling on long journeys.

At the end of Ramadan, houses are decorated with garlands and lights for Eid ul-Fitr to celebrate the end of fasting. Muslims get up very early and go to the mosque, wearing their best clothes, to thank Allah for the self-discipline he has given them during the month of Ramadan. After praying at the mosque, gifts and cards are exchanged at parties and family feasts. Muslims also give money to the poor at Eid ul-Fitr, so that they are also able to enjoy the festival. People say 'Eid Mubarak' to each other, which means 'Happy Festival'. Eid ul-Fitr is all about coming together, and renewing friendships and family ties.

The Islamic calendar is based on lunar months, so Eid ul-Fitr is celebrated when the new moon is seen, signifying the start of the month called Shawwal. This means that the date of the festival varies throughout the western year as the lunar calendar can be around 11 days shorter. It takes place on around the 13th October 2007, 2nd October 2008, 21st September 2009 and 10th September 2010.

Worksheet 1 A comprehension exercise text concerning Ramadan and Eid ul-fitr. The adult will need to have discussed this festival with pupils before they attempt to complete this activity.

Worksheet 2 Two frames with titles, one for each of two picture puzzles.

Worksheet 3 Pieces of two picture puzzles – one representing Ramadan and the other representing Eid ul-

Eid ul-Fitr

Read the text and answer the questions below.

Each year, during the month of Ramadan, all healthy Muslims over the age of twelve fast between dawn and dusk each day. Fasting means having nothing to eat or drink. Muslims fast during Ramadan to remember how the prophet Muhammad was given the sacred texts that now form the Qur'an. Many people go to the mosque to eat together after the sun has set.

The festival of Eid ul-Fitr marks the end of Ramadan. People decorate their houses with garlands and bright lights. It is customary to wear new clothes if possible on the day of the Eid ul-Fitr festival. There are parties and family feasts. All who can afford to will give money, so that the poor and needy are able to enjoy a festive meal too.

A greeting that can often be heard during this festival day is "Eid Mubarak", which means 'happy festival'. This is also seen on greetings cards.

1 What does 'fasting' mean?

_____

_____

2 Would you have to fast during the month of Ramadan? Explain your answer.

_____

_____

3 Which festival marks the end of Ramadan?

_____

_____

4 How might people decorate their homes for this festival?

_____

_____

5 What greeting means 'happy festival'?

_____

_____

Eid ul-Fitr

Name .... Date ....

Cut out the picture pieces on Worksheet 3 as carefully as you can. Arrange the pieces on the grids below so that you create two pictures. The first picture shows what happens during Ramadan. The second picture shows the Eid ul-Fitr festival.

Ramadan

Eid ul-Fitr

Andrew Brodie: Festivals Across the Year 9-11 © A C Black Publishers Ltd. 2007

Eid ul-Fitr

Name .... Date ....

Cut out the puzzle pieces with care. The pieces will make two separate pictures.
The completed puzzles can be stuck into the frames provided on Worksheet 2.

Andrew Brodie: Festivals Across the Year 9-11 © A C Black Publishers Ltd. 2007

Yom Kippur and Sukkot

Teacher's Notes

Background information

Sukkot is one of the three major Jewish festivals (Rosh Hashanah, Yom Kippur and Sukkot), known as the three pilgrim festivals, which celebrate the exodus of the early Jews (or Israelites) who Moses led from slavery in Egypt. It is a joyful festival in which Jews thank God for his provision and protection in the forty years that they spent wandering in the desert on their way to the Promised Land of Israel. Sukkot is traditionally a harvest festival, and a chance to thank God for what he has provided throughout the year.

Sukkot is also known as the 'festival of booths' as Jews mark the festival by building small huts made from natural materials, similar to those that the Israelites made for shelter in the desert. The Torah (the Jewish holy book) gives instructions that after the fields have been harvested there should be seven days of celebration, and that 'all the people of Israel shall live in shelters for seven days, so that your descendents may know that the Lord made the people of Israel live in simple shelters when he led them out of Egypt' (Leviticus 23: 42). This kind of hut or shelter is called a 'sukkah', and has at least three sides and a roof which is partly open to the sky. It is decorated with fruit and vegetables hanging from the ceiling. Whilst nowadays not everyone will build and live in a sukkah for seven days, particularly those in colder countries, where one is built people will often eat meals in it and are supposed to treat it as their home.

Another important ritual which takes place on each day of Sukkot is the ritual waving of the 'Four Species'. The Torah commands Jews to take branches from four plants: the lulav (date palm), hadass (myrtle tree), aravah (willow) and etrog (citron). The waving of these plants usually takes place in the synagogue, and the branches are waved to all four sides, as well as upwards and downwards, while this blessing is recited: 'Blessed are You, God our Lord, King of the Universe, Who has sanctified us with His commandments and commanded us to take the lulav'. These plants are often also used to build the sukkah.

Sukkot usually takes place in the last half of September or the first part of October coming just four days after Yom Kippur (the most solemn day in the Jewish year). It starts on 27th September 2007, 14th October 2008, 3rd October 2009 and 23rd September 2010.

Worksheet 1 helps the pupils to tackle the tricky spelling of the three Jewish festivals.

Worksheet 2 Text with cloze procedure. It is important to discuss these festivals with pupils before asking them to complete this task.

Worksheet 3 Word search with words from all three of the festivals. It is important to discuss these festivals before asking pupils to complete the word search.

Andrew Brodie: Festivals Across the Year 9-11 © A C Black Publishers Ltd. 2007

Yom Kippur and Sukkot

Name .... **Date** ....

Cut out the letters and colour them in. Rearrange them to make the names of the three Jewish pilgrim festivals.

N A R

T K S O

O P M H

Y I A H

S U K U

P A R K

O H H S

Andrew Brodie: Festivals Across the Year 9-11 © A C Black Publishers Ltd. 2007

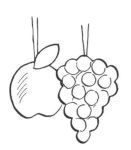

Yom Kippur and Sukkot

Name .... Date ....

Use the words provided to complete the text below.

huts	harvest	desert	adults	sins	week	sides	stars
		remind	blowing	drink	built		

Yom Kippur is the most solemn day in the Jewish calendar. On this day people ask for

forgiveness for their _____ of the previous year. Fasting is an important part of the

day. For twenty-five hours all the healthy _____ go without food and _____ .

When the end of the Yom Kippur fast is signalled by the _____ of a ram's horn,

families enjoy a meal together.

Four days after the very serious Yom Kippur comes the much happier festival of Sukkot.

This festival takes place to celebrate the _____ and to obey God's instructions

that after the harvest there should be seven days of celebration. During this time people should

build huts to live in to _____ them of the years the Israelites spent wandering in

the _____ .

Sometimes this is called the 'Festival of Booths' because of the little _____ that are

built by each family. The huts are only made to last for a _____ . During the week

Jewish people might live in the huts. However, in some countries that would be rather cold, so

families today often just eat some of their meals inside the hut that they have _____ .

The hut that is built has a special name. It is called a 'sukkah' and must be made with at least

three _____ . The roof should be covered with greenery and there should be a space in

the roof so that the _____ can be seen.

Andrew Brodie: Festivals Across the Year 9–11 © A C Black Publishers Ltd 2007

Yom Kippur and Sukkot

Name .... Date ....

✿ The words below can all be found in the word search. They might be horizontal, vertical or diagonal and can be written forwards or backwards.

ROSH HASHANAH	FASTING	SINS	SYNAGOGUE	FORGIVE	WHITE
PRAYERS	YOM KIPPUR	RAM'S HORN	GREENERY	BOOTHS	HUTS
JEWISH	SUKKOT	HARVEST	NEW YEAR		

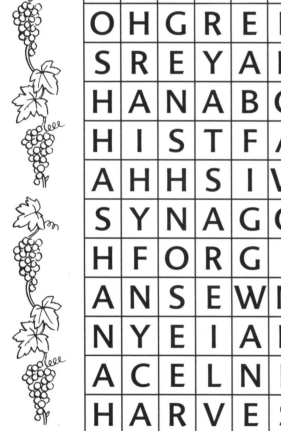

```
R A M'S H O R N R O S Y
O H G R E E N E R Y H O
S R E Y A R P A W S H M
H A N A B O O T H S H K
H I S T F A S T I N G I
A H H S I W E J T E J P
S Y N A G O G U E E W P
H F O R G I V E I S H U
A N S E W N E W Y E A R
N Y E I A R T O K K U S
A C E L N E H U T S B R
H A R V E S T A T I O N
```

When you have shaded all the words write the remaining letters (starting at the top and reading each line left to right) to reveal a message.

___ ___ ___ ___ ___   ___ ___ ___ ___ ___   ___ ___ ___   ___ ___ ___ ___

___ ___ ___ ___ ___ ___   ___ ___ ___ ___   ___ ___ ___ ___

___ ___ ___ ___   ___ ___ ___ ___ ___ ___ ___

Andrew Brodie: Festivals Across the Year 9-11 © A C Black Publishers Ltd. 2007

Diwali

Teacher's Notes

Background information

Diwali (or Divali) is known as the 'festival of lights' and is the most important festival in the Hindu calendar. It celebrates the victory of good over evil and of light over darkness.

Hindus celebrate Diwali for many reasons, but the most common story behind the festival is that of how Rama rescued his wife, Sita, from Ravana, the ten headed demon (see Worksheet 1).

The goddess of wealth, Lakshmi, is also honoured at Diwali. Some Hindus build a shrine to Lakshmi and decorate it with money to thank her for the rewards of wealth they have received. They leave their doors and windows open so that she can enter their houses, and use oil lamps called divas to light the way for her. Brightly coloured symmetrical patterns called rangoli patterns are made on doorsteps from rice to welcome Lakshmi.

Diwali is a joyful festival characterised by decorative lights and diva lamps. People visit relatives, and exchange gifts and cards. There are feasts, parties, joyful festivities and bright firework displays.

Whilst Diwali is thought of mainly as a Hindu festival, it is also celebrated by Sikhs. At Diwali, Sikhs remember when Guru Hargobind, the sixth guru, was released from imprisonment by the Mughal emperor. They also celebrate the laying of the first stone of the Golden Temple at Amritsar, the holiest place in the Sikh world, which took place at Diwali.

Diwali is held in late October or early November. It takes place on 9th November 2007, 28th October 2008, 17th October 2009 and 5th November 2010.

Worksheet 1 Illustrated informative text suitable for guided reading

Worksheet 2 Alphabetical order work

Worksheet 3 Rangoli patterns

Andrew Brodie: Festivals Across the Year 9–11 © A C Black Publishers Ltd 2007

Diwali

Hindus tell the story of Rama and Sita at Diwali.

This is the story of how Rama and his wife Sita were **banished** to the forest for fourteen years. For most of this time they lived there very happily, making friends with the creatures of the forest.

This changed when Ravana, the ten-headed **demon**, captured and **imprisoned** Sita on his island of Lanka.

Rama was a great friend of the monkey general Hanuman and asked for the help of his monkey army. They had many adventures while trying to save Sita, including crossing a bridge formed by the monkeys which stretched all the way to the island. Eventually, Rama rescued Sita and they returned home to live in peace and happiness.

At **Diwali**, brightly coloured **symmetrical** patterns called '**rangoli** patterns' are drawn on doorsteps, to **welcome** Lakshmi, the goddess of peace and **prosperity**, into the home.

Diwali is a joyful festival with many **decorative** lights, including oil lamps called **diva lamps**. At Diwali people visit relatives and exchange gifts and cards. There are feasts, parties, festivities and bright firework displays.

Look at the words in **bold**. You will be using them to complete the next page.

Diwali

Name .... Date ....

The words below need to be sorted into alphabetical order and written on the lines provided. Look at Worksheet 1 first, and if you need any further help, look the words up in a dictionary. Write a definition for each of the words.

Hindus	Diwali	demon	rangoli	diva lamp	banished
prosperity	imprisoned	decorative	symmetrical	welcome	

Words   Definitions

_____   _____

_____   _____

_____   _____

_____   _____

_____   _____

_____   _____

_____   _____

_____   _____

_____   _____

_____   _____

_____   _____

_____   _____

Andrew Brodie: Festivals Across the Year 9–11 © A C Black Publishers Ltd. 2007

Diwali

Name .... Date ....

At Diwali symmetrical rangoli patterns are drawn on doorsteps to welcome Lakshmi (the goddess of peace and prosperity).
Complete this symmetrical pattern. You may add extra pieces to the pattern if you wish to. Use bright colours to colour your work.

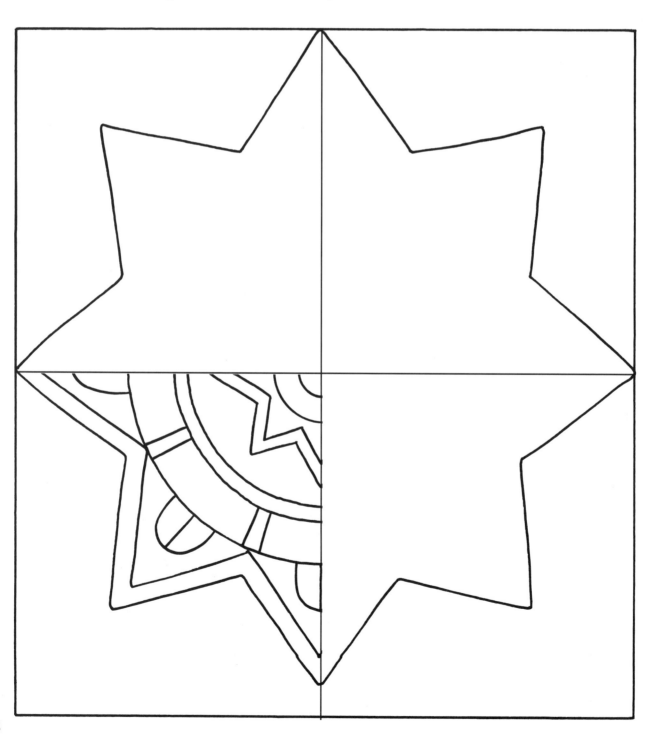

Guru Nanak's Birthday

Teacher's Notes

Background information

Guru Nanak was the first of the ten Sikh gurus, or teachers, of the Sikh faith. Sikhs commemorate many aspects of the gurus' lives, particularly their births and deaths, and they call these occasions 'gurpurbs' (this is sometimes written 'gurpurabs'). Guru Nanak's birthday is the most celebrated gurpurb, and is marked each November or April, depending on whether the lunar or the Nanakshahi (solar) calendar is used to fix the date.

Guru Nanak was the founder of the Sikh religion. He was born in 1469 near Lahore and began his teaching when he was about thirty years old. The area in which he lived was divided between Hindus and Muslims at the time.

Sikhs mark each gurpurb by reading the Guru Granth Sahib (the Sikh holy book which is also regarded as the eleventh and final guru) from beginning to end. This ritual, known as an 'akhand path' takes 48 hours and is done by a team of Sikhs who take it in turns to read sections, ensuring that no gaps or breaks occur in the reading. This usually takes place at gurdwaras (Sikh temple), which are decorated with lights, flowers and flags for the occasion.

Sikhs dress up in their best clothes to go to the gurdwara where they sing hymns from the Guru Granth Sahib and listen to stories and poems about Guru Nanak. In India there are often processions carrying the Guru Granth Sahib through the streets, with singers and martial artists.

Worksheet 1 Some basic information for pupils to read about Guru Nanak and the festival of his birthday. This is a challenging text suitable for higher ability pupils or for other pupils with support.

Worksheet 2 Two stories about Guru Nanak's childhood divided up into paragraphs, to be cut out and rearranged in the right order by groups or individuals.

Worksheet 3 A writing frame on which pupils can write about one of the stories.

Andrew Brodie: Festivals Across the Year 9-11 © A C Black Publishers Ltd 2007

Guru Nanak's Birthday

Read the information below about Sikh festivals. You may need this information to help you to complete the following pages.

A festival for the birthday of a guru is called a 'Gurpurb'. Guru Nanak's birthday is the most popular of these.

Guru Nanak was born in North West India in 1469. At this time, people were either Hindus or Muslims in the area where he lived. He did not think that it was right for people to argue about religion. Guru Nanak believed that God would only care about how people behaved, not about the religion they belonged to. Guru Nanak began to travel around teaching his beliefs. Many people listened and followed his teachings, and this became the start of the Sikh faith.

Guru is a word that means teacher. Guru Nanak was the first of ten human gurus. The eleventh and final guru is a book of songs and poems written by some of the earlier gurus. The book is treated as a guru and is put on a throne when it is being used. The book has a special name: it is called 'Guru Granth Sahib'.

On all the gurpurbs the Guru Granth Sahib is read aloud from beginning to end. It takes about forty-eight hours to do this, so people take turns to read parts of it. The Guru Granth Sahib is also taken out and paraded on the streets. Flags are carried and balloons are held. On Guru Nanak's birthday there may also be processions, with food and drink being given out to spectators.

Guru Nanak told people that everyone was equal. No one was more important than anyone else. He said that everybody should sit together to eat; no one should sit separately because they thought they were more important.

Sikhs all sit together at long tables or on the ground to enjoy a meal when they are celebrating Guru Nanak's Birthday.

Andrew Brodie: Festivals Across the Year 9-11 © A C Black Publishers Ltd. 2007

Guru Nanak's Birthday

Name .... Date ....

These are two of the stories that are told about Guru Nanak's childhood. Cut out the sections and arrange them in the right order to read the stories.

He was told to buy foods that could be sold by the family to make a profit. Nanak's friend Bala went with him.

Even when Guru Nanak was just a boy, he thought a lot about God. One day, his father gave him some money to buy goods from the market.

To everyone's amazement, even though the cattle had spent quite some time in the wrong field no damage had been done and no grass had been eaten.

'What better bargain could there be than feeding the poor?' he said, smiling.

The cattle soon strayed onto a neighbour's field where the grass was rich, green and juicy. The neighbour was upset about this and went to complain to Nanak's father.

Nanak's father was very angry and demanded to know why Nanak hadn't gone home with a good bargain. He was most surprised when Nanak calmly told him that he had got an excellent bargain.

On their way home they again met the holy men. To Bala's surprise, Nanak gave all of the food to the hungry men and returned home with nothing.

On the way to market the two boys passed a group of men praying. They looked very thin and Nanak found out that they had not had anything to eat for days.

At the market Nanak and Bala spent the money that Nanak's father had given them. They bought juicy fresh fruits and crisp ripe vegetables.

When Guru Nanak was a young boy he was sent to look after a field of cattle belonging to his father. Whilst he was with the cattle, instead of watching them carefully, he spent his time thinking about God.

Andrew Brodie: Festivals Across the Year 9–11 © A C Black Publishers Ltd 2007

Guru Nanak's Birthday

Name .... Date ....

On the previous two pages you have found out about the festival held to remember Guru Nanak's birthday, and about two of the stories of the guru as a child.

Choose either a) the customs of the festival or b) one of the stories about the guru. Present one of them as a picture story in the frame below. Use your own words. Make your work as interesting as you can. Illustrate your work with care.

Title:

_____ _____ _____ _____
_____ _____ _____ _____
_____ _____ _____ _____
_____ _____ _____ _____
_____ _____ _____ _____
_____ _____ _____ _____
_____ _____ _____ _____
_____ _____ _____ _____
_____ _____ _____ _____
_____ _____ _____ _____

Hanukkah

Teacher's Notes

Hanukkah is the Jewish Festival of Lights, and is observed by Jews all around the world.

It marks the triumph of a group of Jews, known as the Maccabees, over Antiochus IV, a leader of the Seleucid Empire which succeeded the Empire of Alexander the Great. Jews had lived peacefully under Seleucid rule in Israel for years until Antiochus came to power in around 200BC and persecuted all Jews who continued to practise their faith. He raided the Temple in Jerusalem and ordered an altar to the Greek god Zeus to be built inside. The Jews fought hard to protect their rights and after three years of fighting the Maccabees triumphed. The Temple was reclaimed and rededicated.

Olive oil was needed to light the menorah, a seven-branched candelabrum which was kept constantly alight in the Temple. The Maccabees could only find enough oil to keep the eternal flame burning for one day. Miraculously, the existing oil continued to burn for not one, but eight days whilst the long task of preparing and consecrating more oil was being carried out. The word Hanukkah means dedication, as the festival marks the rededication of the Temple, and it lasts for eight days to commemorate the Miracle of the Oil.

A special nine-branched menorah is used by Jews to mark Hanukkah, with a central candle which is higher than the four candles to either side. In the evening prior to each day of the festival, prayers are said while the central candle is used to light the other candles. One is lit for the first day, two are lit for the second day, and so on. Children may be given small gifts at the time the candles are lit.

Hanukkah traditions include eating foods that are fried in oil, such as potato latkes (a type of fried potato cake) and sufganiot (jam doughnut), to remember the Miracle of the Oil. Children often play games with a dreidel (a four-sided spinning top), used by Jews in the time when they had to meet together to worship in secret. They would hide their Torah scrolls and pretend to be playing with a dreidel whenever any guards discovered them.

Hanukkah usually takes place in December, but occasionally falls in late November or early January.

Worksheet 1 Cloze procedure information text. It is important that an adult discusses the festival with pupils before this activity is tackled.

Worksheet 2 Pictures of artefacts for writing about.

Worksheet 3 Information and instructions for playing Dreidel.

Hanukkah

Use the words from the box to complete the text about Hanukkah.

December	temple	oil	gifts	eating	playing	lit	worship
	burning	candles		eight	Jews		

The festival of Hanukkah usually takes place in _____ . It lasts for eight days and is also known as the Festival of Lights.

The festival celebrates a story that took place around two thousand two hundred years ago. At that time the Jews were forbidden to _____ God in the way they liked. They had to fight to protect their ways of worship and after three years they managed to win back a temple in Jerusalem that had been taken from them.

Oil was needed to light the Menorah in the _____ but there only seemed to be enough to keep it _____ for one day. Whilst the long task of fetching more oil was being carried out, the existing oil continued to burn for not one, but _____ days.

Hanukkah traditions include _____ particular fried foods. This is because frying uses _____ , which is important in the story. Two popular foods during this festival are 'potato latkes' (a type of fried potato cake) and 'sufganiot' (jam doughnut).

Another tradition is playing 'Dreidel'. This comes from the time when _____ were not allowed to meet together to worship. Dreidel is a game played with a type of small spinning top. When they met they had the game with them, so that if an official came by they could pretend to be _____ this game.

The Menorah (candlestick) used for Hanukkah is a special one, with eight branches and a central branch that is higher than the four on either side. The candle in the middle is only used to light the other _____ .

This type of Menorah used for Hanukkah is called a Hanukiyah. Each evening during the festival one candle is _____ and prayers are said. Children may be given little _____ each time a candle is lit. These gifts are often small amounts of money. One candle is added to the Hanukiyah each night so that by the end of the festival they are all alight.

Andrew Brodie: Festivals Across the Year 9–11 © A C Black Publishers Ltd. 2007

Hanukkah

Name .... Date ....

Look at the pictures below.
Each picture shows an item that is remembered during the Hanukkah festival.
Label each picture and write a sentence or two to explain it. Now colour the pictures.

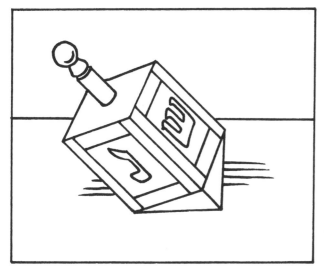

_____

_____

_____

_____

_____

_____

Andrew Brodie: Festivals Across the Year 9–11 © A C Black Publishers Ltd 2007

Hanukkah

Name .... Date ....

The game of Dreidel.

☆ The dreidel is a type of spinning top with rectangular sides. The dreidel was originally made of clay but modern ones are usually wood or plastic. Cut out the net of the shape (shown below) and make one from card.

The four sides of the dreidel are each marked with a Hebrew letter, Nun, Gimmel, Ileh and Shin. They stand for the words in the Hebrew phrase 'Nes Gadol Hayah Sham' meaning a great miracle happened, which refers to the burning of the oil for eight days. The four letters also stand for the words that mean nothing, all, half and put, these being the instructions to follow when spinning the dreidel.

The game can be played using the instructions below.

Equipment   A dreidel   Coloured counters (10 per player)

Instructions   Play this game with 2, 3 or 4 players.
Each person puts one counter in the middle.
Take turns to spin the dreidel.
If it lands on 'nit' (nothing) nothing happens and the next player has his/her turn.
If it lands on 'gantz' (all) the player takes all the counters from the centre.
If it lands on 'halb' (half) the player takes half the counters.
If it lands on 'shtell' (put) the player adds one to the middle.

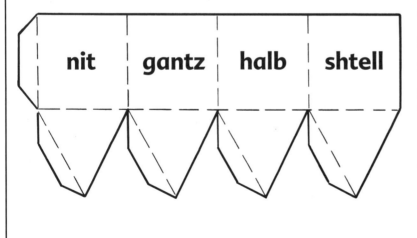

When the middle area has no counters each player must put one in before the game continues.
The game ends when one player has all the counters. An alternative ending can be to see which player has the most counters after a set amount of time. Decide on the time (5 or 10 minutes) before you start playing. Use a stopwatch.

Andrew Brodie: Festivals Across the Year 9–11 © A C Black Publishers Ltd. 2007

26

Christmas

Teacher's Notes

Background information

Christmas is when Christians celebrate the birth of Jesus Christ. Jesus was the founder of Christianity, and Christians believe that he was the Son of God.

The Christmas story is known as the Nativity. It says that an angel visited a young woman called Mary, and told her that she was going to have a baby boy who would be the Son of God and that she must call him Jesus. At the time, there was a census taking place, and Mary was required to travel with her fiancé, Joseph, to his home town of Bethlehem. They couldn't find anywhere to stay, but an inn-keeper offered them shelter in his stable, and this is where Jesus was born. Shepherds were called to the scene by angels, and wise men from the East, bringing precious gifts, followed a bright new star to the stable after hearing a prophecy that it would lead to a new king.

Families traditionally put up a Christmas tree in their homes in the weeks leading up to Christmas. The tree is then decorated with lights, tinsel and baubles. Homes, schools, shops and offices are also often decorated. On Christmas Day, greetings cards and gifts are exchanged, and a family meal is enjoyed.

Christians go to church on Christmas morning, and some attend a service at midnight the night before, called midnight mass. Christmas carols and hymns are sung and prayers are said for peace and goodwill.

As with many religious festivals, Christmas traditions vary in different countries across the world. Christmas takes place on 25th December.

Worksheet 1 A short text for pupils to read.

Worksheet 2 A Christmas word puzzle with clues to answers that can be found on Worksheet 1.

Worksheet 3 A Christmas word search.

Andrew Brodie: Festivals Across the Year 9-11 © A C Black Publishers Ltd. 2007

Christmas

Christmas is a Christian festival that takes place on 25th December each year and celebrates the birth of Jesus Christ. Christians believe that Christ was not a human being, but the Son of God. Jesus Christ is also referred to in the Bible as the Messiah, meaning the one chosen to save the world.

His mother Mary, now also called the Madonna, was told by the angel Gabriel that she would give birth to a baby boy. Mary lived in Nazareth but because a census was taking place she had to travel to Bethlehem with Joseph, the man she was going to marry, because this was his home town.

As Mary and Joseph could find nowhere to stay, the baby was born in a stable, and a manger was used as a cradle. A manger is a trough that would normally be filled with food for the animals.

Wise men from the East followed a new star, having heard a prophecy that this would lead to a new king. These men, known as the Magi or the three kings, are thought to have been called Melchior, Balthazar and Caspar.

The wise men carried gifts of gold, frankincense and myrrh. These were very precious gifts, fit for a king. When Herod, the king of Judea, found out about this, he was worried that this new king would try to take his place. He asked the Magi to tell him the whereabouts of the new king when they had found him. He pretended that this was so that he could also take a gift, but it was really so that he could kill the new infant king.

After finding the baby and presenting their gifts, an angel visited the Magi and told them to return to their country by a different route to avoid meeting King Herod.

Although the visit of the kings is often celebrated at Christmas, it did not happen on the same day as the birth and is officially celebrated on 6th January (Epiphany).

The twenty-four days leading up to Christmas day are called Advent. This is a time when Christians prepare for the Christmas celebrations. During this time special church services are held, homes are decorated and greetings cards are exchanged.

 # Christmas

Name .... Date ....

Use the information in Worksheet 1 to help you answer the following clues.

Clue ⟡ ⭐ ⟡ ⭐ ⟡ ⭐ ⟡ ⭐   **Answer** ⟡ ⭐ ⟡ ⭐

1. The twenty four days leading up to Christmas   A _____

2. Another name for the three wise men   M _____

3. A Christian place of worship   C _____

4. A title for Mary the mother of Jesus   M _____

5. Jesus Christ was known as this   M _____

6. The names of the three Magi   C _____
   M _____
   B _____

7. The gifts they gave to Jesus   G _____
   F _____
   M _____

8. This was used as a cradle for the baby   M _____

9. The day when the visit of the Magi is celebrated   E _____

10. The king who wanted to kill the baby Jesus   H _____

Andrew Brodie: Festivals Across the Year 9-11 © A C Black Publishers Ltd 2007

Christmas

Name .... Date ....

Shade the words in the word search below.

ADVENT	ANGEL GABRIEL	BALTHAZAR	BETHLEHEM	CASPAR	CHURCH
FRANKINCENSE	HEROD	EPIPHANY	JOSEPH	MADONNA	MANGER
MELCHIOR	MESSIAH	MYRRH	NATIVITY	NAZARETH	SHEPHERD	STABLE

J	O	S	E	P	H	S	T	A	B	L	E	C	N
B	H	M	A	D	O	N	N	A	Q	S	P	R	A
E	I	S	X	Q	T	I	X	A	N	N	I	R	Z
T	S	R	O	I	H	C	L	E	M	C	P	E	A
H	E	T	L	E	B	R	C	A	T	E	H	G	R
L	C	N	H	R	I	N	A	S	T	M	A	N	E
E	A	E	S	O	I	N	S	T	H	E	N	A	T
H	M	V	T	K	X	W	P	E	N	T	Y	M	H
E	Y	D	N	Y	F	N	A	T	I	V	I	T	Y
M	R	A	I	F	T	H	R	H	C	R	U	H	C
O	R	F	Q	D	M	E	S	S	I	A	H	E	C
F	H	B	A	L	T	H	A	Z	A	R	E	Q	M
A	N	G	E	L	G	A	B	R	I	E	L	B	E
D	O	R	E	H	R	D	R	E	H	P	E	H	S

Now shade all the Qs and Xs.
Reading the remaining letters from right to left beginning on the top row you will find a message. Write the message in the spaces below.

__ __ __ __ __ __   __ __ __ __ __ __   __ __ __ __

__ __ __ __ __ __ __ __ __   __ __   __ __ __ __ __

__ __ __ __ __   __ __ __ __ __ __ __ __ .

Chinese New Year

Teacher's Notes

Background information

Chinese New Year is the most important date in the Chinese calendar. It is also sometimes known as the Spring Festival and is considered a major holiday in China and other countries that are greatly influenced by Chinese culture, such as Mongolia, Tibet, Vietnam, Bhutan, Korea and Nepal. It is celebrated by Chinese communities across the world.

Chinese New Year is a time of parties and celebrations, of visiting friends and family to wish them good luck and prosperity in the coming year, and of much Chinese symbolism. In the days leading up to New Year, houses are thoroughly cleaned to sweep out bad luck, and just before midnight on New Year's Eve, doors and windows are left open to allow the old year to leave and the new year to enter. Brooms and mops must be put away before New Year arrives, to welcome good luck into the house and ensure that it is not swept away.

On New Year's Day, many celebrations and parades take place. Brightly coloured flags and banners are waved, and fireworks are let off to frighten away evil spirits. Big colourful dragons often take part in the parade, as dragons are a symbol of good luck, and dancers dressed as lions welcome in the new year, as lions are considered guardians.

People will leave their homes to watch the parades and to give New Year greetings to their neighbours, family and friends. New Year gifts of money are given to younger family members in red envelopes, as red symbolises good things and is a sign of good luck. Red is widely associated with Chinese New Year, with many houses being decorated in red and children often wearing new red clothes.

The kind of food eaten at New Year is also heavily influenced by Chinese symbolism. Foods will often be eaten because their Chinese name sounds similar to common New Year greetings and wishes. Chinese dumplings are eaten because they look like gold nuggets, so they are thought of as an omen of prosperity.

The end of the New Year period is marked fifteen days later with the Lantern Festival. At this time people decorate homes and streets with lanterns and there are more fireworks and dragon parades.

Chinese New Year is based on the lunar calendar, and is usually celebrated in late January or early February.

Worksheet 1 Information text for reading and discussion - the information will be needed to complete Worksheet 2.

Worksheet 2 A design activity based on the information from the text.

Worksheet 3 A picture puzzle to be reassembled and coloured.

Andrew Brodie: Festivals Across the Year 9-11 © A C Black Publishers Ltd. 2007

Chinese New Year

Read the text below about Chinese New Year. It will help you with the tasks on the following pages.

Chinese New Year takes place in late January or early February. There is a cycle of twelve years, with each one named after a different animal. A traditional story tells how the years were named: the animals took part in a race across a river and the years are named in the order the animals reached the opposite bank.

Below is a list of the animals, with some of their year dates. To find out which other years belong to each animal simply add or subtract twelve or multiples of twelve.

Dragon	2000	Snake	2001
Horse	2002	Ram	2003
Monkey	2004	Cockerel	2005
Dog	2006	Pig	2007
Rat	2008	Ox	2009
Tiger	2010	Hare	2011

In the days before New Year, houses are thoroughly cleaned and just before midnight on New Year's Eve the doors and windows are opened to allow the old year to leave and the new one to enter.

As part of the celebration, fireworks are let off. These are to frighten away evil spirits.

On New Year's Day people will leave their homes to give New Year greetings to their neighbours, family and friends.

The Dragon is a symbol of good luck, so New Year parades will often include dragon dancing. The colour red is also considered lucky so New Year gifts of money will be placed in lucky red envelopes.

The end of the New Year period is marked fifteen days later by the lantern festival. At this time lanterns decorate homes and streets, and again there are fireworks and dragon dancing.

Andrew Brodie: Festivals Across the Year 9–11 © A C Black Publishers Ltd. 2007

Chinese New Year

Name .... Date ....

Design a Chinese New Year poster.

You have been given a wheel in the centre to help you show the cycle of years. You should include at least two 'dated' years for each of the animals.

Try and work out the animal sign years in which some of your family or children in different years at your school were born. You might also want to include pictures representing New Year customs.

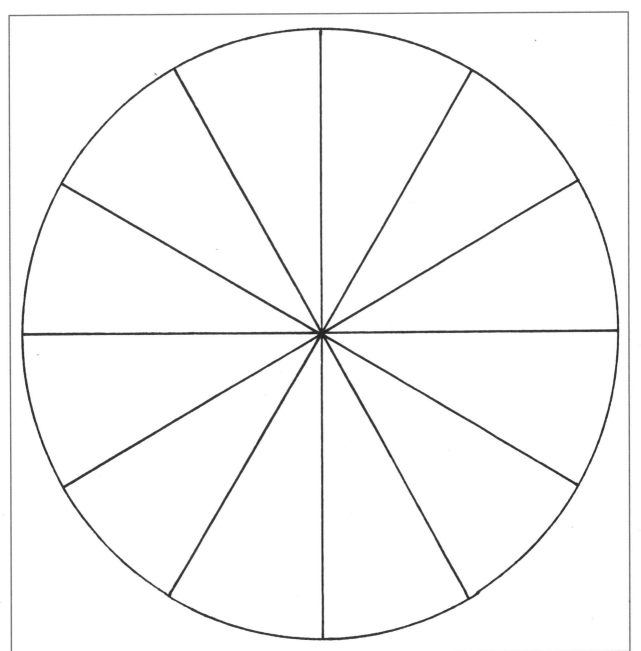

Andrew Brodie: Festivals Across the Year 9-11 © A C Black Publishers Ltd. 2007

Chinese New Year

Name .... Date ....

✿ Cut out the pieces below and put them together on another sheet of paper to form a Chinese New Year picture.
Colour your picture carefully. Remember that red is a lucky colour.

Holi

Teacher's Notes

Background information

Holi is celebrated by Hindus in India and all across the world. It is marked on the day after the full moon during the month of Phalunga, which usually falls in March but occasionally in late February, and it celebrates the start of spring and the new life that is associated with it. Holi is an energetic, fun-filled festival with an overwhelming spirit of good humour and goodwill.

Holi commemorates the story of Holika, sister of the demon king, who was burned to death in a fire that had been intended to kill the king's son, Prahlad (this is sometimes written Prahlada). (See Worksheet 1 for the full story of Holika). On the evening before Holi, bonfires are lit in the streets in India, and coconuts are roasted in the flames to remember the story. In some parts of India, a model of Holika is thrown onto the bonfire. The message of the story is of good winning over evil and of the god Vishnu's protection of those who are faithful to him.

While the origins of Holi are rooted in religious stories, there are no major religious rituals which should be performed during the festival. Holi is also known as the Festival of Colour, as people throw brightly coloured powders or coloured water at each other and at passers by, shouting 'Don't feel offended, it's Holi!' It is a very messy affair as people are drenched in coloured water, and the air is filled with all the coloured powder. The feeling of goodwill at Holi is reinforced as differences of caste, wealth, gender and age are put aside. Everyone is so colourful that it is difficult to tell who is rich and who is poor!

Holi is also a time of singing and dancing, and in the evening friends and families eat big celebratory meals together to round off the festivities.

Practical Activity

This activity can be great fun on a warm day but you should ask for parents' permission first. You will obviously have to take account of Health and Safety issues. Have buckets of water each coloured a different colour with a little food colouring. Ask pupils to bring a change of clothes (old shorts and t-shirt are ideal), a towel and a water pistol. Mark out an area of the playground in which the children can soak each other, leaving those outside the area clean and dry, and recreate Holi by squirting the coloured water at each other. It is better if a member of staff joins in to help reinforce the notion that children are allowed to throw their powders or coloured water at adults during Holi.

Worksheet 1 Information for pupils to read concerning the festival of Holi.

Worksheet 2 Comprehension task based on information found in Worksheet 1. The answers are: Holi, India, bonfires, water, gulal, energy, joy, king, Hiranyakashipu, Holika, face, bura na mano, Holi hai.

Worksheet 3 Word puzzle based on information on Worksheet 1. The answers to this puzzle are:
1) Holi, 2) spring, 3) bura no mano, Holi hai, 4) water, 5) bonfires, 6) joy, 7) flames, 8) Krishna, 9) India, 10) worship, 11) Radha 12) Holika, 13) Prahlad, 14) Gulal.
The answer found in the shaded vertical column is Hiranyakashipu.

Andrew Brodie: Festivals Across the Year 9-11 © A C Black Publishers Ltd 2007

Holi

Read the information below about the Hindu festival of Holi.

The ancient festival of Holi originally took place in India to give thanks for the arrival of spring and the first harvests of the year. Hindus throughout the world now enjoy it and there are many different fun Holi rituals and customs.

One important feature of the Holi festival is the lighting of a large bonfire. There are public bonfires in each community, and there may be singing, dancing, story-telling, the roasting of coconuts or grains in the flames, eating specially made sweets and much general merrymaking. There may also be processions with a carnival atmosphere.

People also have lots of fun drenching friends and relatives by squirting them with coloured water or throwing coloured powders (known as 'gulal') at them. It is believed that the bright colours used signify energy, joy and life.

There are also a number of legends that are associated with the festival of Holi. Two of the main ones are outlined below.

One famous story is that of the demon king Hiranyakashipu. He wanted to kill his son, the prince Prahlad, as the boy refused to obey his father's command to worship him and prayed to the Lord Vishnu instead. The furious king tried, and failed, a number of times to kill him. The final attempt involved the king's evil sister Holika, who was immune to fire if she entered it alone. She pulled Prahlad into the flames of a bonfire with her, only to lose her protection and burn to death in the flames whilst Prahlad survived unharmed because the god Vishnu protected him.

Another tale often told at Holi is thought to be the origin of the custom of throwing colours at one another. It is the legend of Lord Krishna who, as a young man, loved a girl called Radha. He told his mother how unfair he felt it was that he had a dark complexion whilst Radha had a very fair one. His mother, Yashoda, suggested that he should find out what Radha would look like with a darker appearance by colouring her face any colour he liked and he decided to follow her advice. It is easy to see how this story led to the throwing of coloured waters and powders during Holi.

If you are ever lucky enough to be part of the spring festival of Holi, you might hear someone shouting 'bura na mano, Holi hai', meaning 'don't be cross, it's Holi'. Be warned: around the same time as you hear this, you might suddenly find yourself dripping in coloured water or covered in brightly coloured powders!

Andrew Brodie: Festivals Across the Year 9-11 © A C Black Publishers Ltd. 2007

Holi

Name .... Date ....

Fill the places in the sentences below. Use the information on Worksheet 1 to help you. Make sure you spell the words correctly. In some places there are small picture clues to help you.

The Hindu festival of _____ is celebrated each year in spring.

This festival originated in _____ and is now celebrated by Hindus throughout the world.

Large public _____ are built and these are lit on the first evening of the festival.

People throw coloured powders and squirt _____ at one another.

The brightly coloured powders are called _____ .

These bright colours used are said to represent life, _____ and _____ .

One story told at Holi is about a demon _____ called _____ who tries to kill his son.

His wicked sister _____ ends up burning in the flames.

Another story is about Lord Krishna wanting to change the colour of Radha's _____ .

During Holi people often shout '_____ _____ , _____ _____ ' meaning 'don't be angry, it's Holi'.

Andrew Brodie: Festivals Across the Year 9–11 © A C Black Publishers Ltd 2007

Holi

Name .... Date ....

Write the answers to the clues in the spaces provided.
If your answers are correct the name of the demon king should be in the shaded column. Write the name in the space beneath the quiz.

1) The Hindu spring festival.

2) The season in which the festival is celebrated.

3) You might hear this called out when you are suddenly soaked.

4) This could be squirted at you.

5) These are lit on the first evening of Holi.

6) The bright colours represent this.

7) These burned Holika.

8) Radha was loved by him.

9) The country where the festival of Holi originated.

10) The demon king believed everyone should _____ him.

11) Lord Krishna loved her.

12) The name of the demon king's evil sister.

13) The name of the king's son.

14) The brightly coloured powders are called _____.

The name of the demon king was:

__ __ __ __ __ __ __ __ __ __ __ __ .

Andrew Brodie: Festivals Across the Year 9-11 © A C Black Publishers Ltd. 2007

Pesach

Teacher's Notes

Pesach, or Passover, is the most anticipated festival in the Jewish calendar and is celebrated by Jews everywhere. It takes place in March or April and it lasts for seven days in Israel and eight days elsewhere.

Pesach celebrates the exodus of the Israelites from slavery in ancient Egypt, under the leadership of Moses. Jews believe that God sent Moses to ask Pharaoh to release the Israelites from Egypt, but Pharaoh refused. God then gave Moses the power to release a series of plagues, which killed many Egyptians and all Egyptian livestock. Before inflicting the tenth and final plague, God told the Israelites to slaughter a lamb and smear its blood on their door frames. They were then to roast the lamb and eat it with bitter herbs, and be ready for a long journey. Jews commemorate this meal at Pesach.

The final plague was the death of every firstborn son in Egypt, but the plague 'passed over' all the houses which had lamb's blood smeared on the door frame. This is where the name 'Passover' comes from. Once this plague had hit, the Egyptians pleaded with Pharaoh to banish the Israelites from Egypt. He agreed and the Israelites fled, taking their bread with them which had not had time to rise. While fleeing through the desert they ate this unleavened bread, and for this reason only unleavened bread (Matzah) is allowed during the festival of Pesach.

Any foods that contain yeast as a rising agent are not permitted for the duration of the festival, and Jewish houses must be thoroughly cleaned and cleared out before Pesach to ensure that none of these foods, or anything that has been used to prepare them are in the house. Special sets of crockery and cutlery are reserved for use during Passover only.

The Pesach meal, or the Seder, includes many practices which must all be carried out in a specific order and contain much symbolism from the Pesach story. The meal can take several hours to complete. The Seder plate is a specially decorated plate for the following items:

A roasted shankbone (A reminder of

the lamb sacrificed on the night of the Passover)

Bitter herbs (To represent the bitterness of slavery)

A roasted egg (A reminder of the cycle of life)

Haroset (A paste made from apples, walnuts, cinnamon and wine that represents the mortar used by the Israelite slaves in Egypt)

Karpas (A green vegetable dipped in salt water to represent the tears of the Jewish slaves)

Worksheet 1 Information about Pesach – this will be needed to complete sheets C and D.

Worksheet 2 This asks pupils to label a picture of a Seder plate.

Worksheet 3 Pesach word puzzle. Answers: 1A) Saltwater 1D) Seder 2A) Haggadah 2D) Hail 3A) Locusts 3D) Lamb 4A) Egypt 4D) Egg 5A) Plagues 5D) Parsley 6A) Flies 6D) Frogs 7A) Bitter herbs 7D) Boils 8A) Prophet 8D) Pesach.

Andrew Brodie: Festivals Across the Year 9-11 © A C Black Publishers Ltd. 2007

Pesach

Read the information on this page. It will help you with the next worksheet.

Pesach is the name for the Passover festival celebrated by members of the Jewish religion. It is held in the spring, and celebrates the delivery from slavery of the Israelites in ancient Egypt.

In preparation for the festival, houses must be thoroughly cleaned and all traces of food containing certain grains and yeast must be thrown away. This is to remember that when the Israelites fled from Egypt, they left in such a rush that they did not have time to let their bread rise before they cooked it. During the festival, special biscuits called matzos, made from flour and water, are eaten instead of bread.

A family meal is a very important feature of Pesach. This meal can last for several hours, as there are certain things that must be done during the meal. The youngest member of the family has to ask some set questions. The head of the family gives the set answers to these questions. The order in which things have to be done and said are given in a book called the Haggadah.

An important part of the meal is the Seder plate. On the Seder plate are special items: bitter herbs, parsley, egg, lamb bone, haroset (a mixture of finely chopped nuts, apples, wine and cinnamon) and salt water. The salt water is a reminder of the tears of the slaves. The haroset is made into a paste and brings to mind the mortar used by the Israelite slaves when they were forced to build Egyptian houses. Bitter herbs represent the bitterness of slavery. The lamb bone signifies the lambs that were sacrificed on the eve of the departure from Egypt. Parsley (or lettuce) is a reminder of springtime and new hope for the future. Finally, the egg symbolizes the cycle of life.

The story that is remembered at Passover is how God helped a prophet called Moses to lead the Israelites out of Egypt. The Israelites were slaves in Egypt and God told Moses to follow his instructions to secure their release. Moses warned the Egyptian king that if they were not released the River Nile would turn to blood. The king refused, so the Nile was turned to blood. Each time the king refused to release the slaves, another plague was sent: a plague of frogs, one of gnats, one of flies, then a disease that killed the Egyptian animals, a plague of boils, then another of hail, one of locusts, three days of darkness and lastly the Passover itself. This time, the Israelite slaves had to kill lambs to eat and mark the doors of their houses with lamb's blood. That night, the firstborn male of each Egyptian family was killed, but the homes with blood on the doors were 'passed over' and their children survived. After this, the king allowed the slaves a very short time to escape before trying to catch them again. God parted the Red Sea to allow the Israelites to pass across safely, but let the sea come together again to drown the Egyptians who were chasing them.

Andrew Brodie: Festivals Across the Year 9–11 © A C Black Publishers Ltd. 2007

Pesach

Name .... Date ....

Look at the picture below.
Label each of the items and explain why it is there.

Andrew Brodie: Festivals Across the Year 9-11 © A C Black Publishers Ltd. 2007

Pesach

Name .... Date ....

Complete the word puzzles below.

1

1 Across A reminder of tears.

1 Down Plate used at Pesach meal.

2

2 Across Book of instructions for the Pesach meal.

2 Down _ _ _ _ stones fell on the Egyptians.

3

3 Across A plague of these ate crops.

3 Down A bone from this is on the Seder plate.

4

4 Across The country where the Israelites were enslaved.

4 Down A reminder of the cycle of life.

5

5 Across These were suffered by the Egyptians.

5 Down A reminder of spring and future hope.

6

6 Across These flew around Egypt.

6 Down These jumped out of the river.

7

7 Across These represent the bitterness of slavery.

7 Down This plague made Egyptian people and animals very sore.

8

8 Across Moses was one of these.

8 Down The Passover festival.

Easter

Teacher's Notes

Easter is the most important Christian festival as it celebrates the resurrection of Jesus Christ from the dead, the event which forms the basis of Christianity itself. It is celebrated by all Christians in March or early April each year.

In the weeks before Easter, Christians remember the events leading up to the death and resurrection of Jesus. Lent is the period of forty days (excluding Sundays) before Easter; it is traditionally a time of prayer and fasting before the celebrations on Easter Day. Nowadays, Christians often give up something they enjoy for these forty days, instead of fasting.

Palm Sunday is the Sunday before Easter, on which Christians remember when Jesus rode into Jerusalem on a donkey to the adulation of the crowds who made a carpet of palm leaves in front of him. They also think about Christ and his disciples eating the Last Supper together as Jesus foretold his betrayal by Judas to the Roman guards and his execution for blasphemy.

The main focus of the festival is on the Easter weekend. Good Friday is a time of reflection and prayer as Christians remember when Jesus was crucified by the Romans. They believe that Jesus died to take the blame for the sins of all Christians, but that he rose from the dead on the Sunday and appeared to some of his disciples. This is what Christians celebrate on Easter Sunday.

Easter is a spring festival and as such has connections with new life. For this reason, chocolate eggs are often given to children on Easter Sunday.

Worksheet 1 Information text. It is important to discuss this text with pupils to ensure their understanding of it.

Worksheet 2/3 These two sheets can be photocopied back to back to form an A5 sized Easter booklet for pupils to complete.

Andrew Brodie: Festivals Across the Year 9-11 © A C Black Publishers Ltd 2007

Easter

Easter is the most important Christian festival. Christians believe that Jesus Christ was killed and that two days later he rose again from the dead. Easter Sunday is the end of a week known as Holy Week.

Holy Week begins on Palm Sunday when Jesus is said to have ridden into Jerusalem on a donkey. Crowds lined the streets and palm leaves were strewn ahead of him to form a carpet.

The following Thursday, called 'Maundy Thursday', is when 'the Last Supper' is remembered. The Last Supper was the final Passover meal that Jesus had with his twelve disciples. Jesus knew that one of his disciples would soon betray him and hand him over to the Roman authorities to be killed. The Romans considered Jesus a troublemaker because of the way in which he spoke about his beliefs and claimed to be the Son of God.

'Good Friday' is the following day. This is a solemn day, as it remembers that Jesus was nailed to a large cross to die. This is also known as crucifixion.

The final day of Holy Week is Easter Sunday. This is a very joyful occasion, as Christians believe that on this day Jesus rose from the dead. The cave in which his body had been put was empty and at the entrance was an angel. For Christians, it is through Jesus's death and resurrection that people's broken relationship with God is restored. They believe that Jesus died to take the punishment for all the things that they have done wrong, so that they can then be forgiven by God and try to live better lives.

In Great Britain there are two days when most places of work are closed to celebrate Easter. These are Good Friday and the day after Easter Sunday, which is known as Easter Monday.

On Easter Sunday, cards and chocolate eggs may be given to one another. The reason that eggs have become a symbol of the Easter festival is because they represent new life. This is linked to the Christian belief in the resurrection and also because Easter is a spring festival when the natural world is full of new life.

> **Make your own information booklet about Easter using the information from the text and anything else you have learned about this festival. The booklet (Worksheets 2 and 3) has been provided for you to complete.**
>
> **Write neatly and with correct spellings. Illustrate your work with care.**

Easter

Author

Easter Customs

Good Friday

Easter Sunday

Palm Sunday

Maundy Thursday

Baisakhi

Teacher's Notes

Background information

Baisakhi is a religious festival which celebrates the beginning of the Sikh religion as it is known today. Long before Baisakhi took on new significance for the Sikh faith it had been celebrated as the Punjabi New Year and the first day of the harvest in the Punjab region of India. Crowds would gather at Keshgarh Sahib near Anandpur to mark the beginning of the year, to hope for a good harvest season, and to listen to the guru.

Guru Teg Bahadur was the ninth Sikh guru. In 1657 the Mughal Emperor, Aurangzeb, declared himself the Emperor of India and tried to make all of India Muslim. He persecuted Hindus and Sikhs, so Guru Teg Bahadur made his young son, Gobind Rai, the tenth guru and went to Delhi to try to end the suffering of the Hindus and Sikhs. Guru Teg Bahadur was seized by Aurangzeb and executed. His body was left in a heap after the execution, but not a single Sikh was brave enough to step forward and claim the body so that religious rites could be performed on it for fear that he too would be killed.

Guru Gobind Rai was angered by this and in 1699 he called for Sikhs from far and wide to make a special effort to attend the Baisakhi celebrations at Keshgarh Sahib. He wanted to raise the spirits of the downtrodden Sikhs and give them a strong identity in the face of this persecution, and did this by initiating the community of Khalsa. Hundreds of thousands of people gathered as the guru made a long

and emotive speech about the need for a spirit of courage and sacrifice, like that of his father. This sets the scene for the story of Baisakhi on Worksheet 1.

On the day of Baisakhi, Sikhs gather early at their Gurdwaras for a special prayer meeting. Five Sikhs who represent the Five Beloved Ones of the Baisakhi story read the same verses that were read in 1699. Everyone is given amrit to sip and devotes themselves to the community of Khalsa. Religious songs are sung before everyone takes part in a community lunch known as guru-ka-langar. Later in the day, the Sikh holy book which is also thought of as the final guru, the Guru Granth Sahib, is processed through the streets as people chant and sing.

In the Punjab region of India, Baisakhi is also still remembered as a harvest festival and is often celebrated with traditional bhangra and gidda dancing. Baisakhi usually falls on April 13th, but once every 36 years it falls on April 14th.

Worksheet 1 Information text suitable for guided reading. This could be used as a classroom or assembly activity.

Worksheet 2 Writing activity based on the text on Worksheet 1.

Worksheet 3 Creating a word search about Baisakhi.

Andrew Brodie: Festivals Across the Year 9-11 © A C Black Publishers Ltd. 2007

47

Baisakhi

Read about the festival of Baisakhi

The festival of Baisakhi is held on 13th April each year. It celebrates the New Year, the growing of crops and the harvest. Special dancing called 'Bhangra' is often seen at this festival. Bhangra is a type of dancing that tells the story of the harvest from the seeds being sown to the crops being gathered in. It is very cheerful; drummers play exciting rhythms and the dancers wear bright costumes.

Baisakhi is also the day when all people who wish to follow the Sikh faith take part in the ceremony of Amrit. Amrit is a drink that contains sugar and water and is made in a special way. People who wish to take part in this ceremony must be wearing the five Ks of the Sikh religion. The five Ks are: Kes (hair that is not cut), Kanga, (a comb), Kirpan (a sword with a curved blade), Kara (a bangle worn on the wrist of the right hand) and Kachh (a pair of cotton shorts).

The reason for this part of the Baisakhi festival is because of an event that happened on Baisakhi day in 1699. At that time when thousands of Sikhs had gathered for the festival, the Guru Gobind Singh asked the crowd if there was any Sikh there who would give up his life for God. There was one volunteer and he was led away by the guru. When Guru Gobind Singh returned, the crowd were shocked to see his sword was covered with blood.

The guru asked for another person who was willing to give his life for God and after a while another volunteer stepped forward. He was also led away, out of the sight of the crowd, and again the guru returned with a blood-soaked sword. This continued until five people had been taken.

The guru then returned with all five men still healthy and in good spirits. No one had been killed. It had been a test of faith and courage. These were the first Sikhs who took 'Amrit' and the first who were told to wear the five Ks.

Baisakhi is a very happy day and after meeting and praying in the Gurdwara (the building where Sikhs meet and pray) they will all eat a meal together.

Andrew Brodie: Festivals Across the Year 9–11 © A C Black Publishers Ltd. 2007

Baisakhi

Name .... Date ....

Write a sentence (or two) in your own words to accompany each of the pictures below. The text on Worksheet 1 has all the information you need to complete this task.

_____
_____
_____
_____
_____
_____

_____
_____
_____
_____
_____
_____

_____
_____
_____
_____
_____
_____

_____
_____
_____
_____
_____
_____

Baisakhi

Name .... Date ....

Use the frame below to make a word search.
The words may be written horizontally, vertically or diagonally, and may be forwards or backwards. Use capital letters.

The 18 words that must be included in your word search are shown in the box.

When you have included all the words, fill the other spaces with extra letters.

Ask a friend to do your word search.

GURU	AMRIT	KES	KANGA	KIRPAN	BAISAKHI	VOLUNTEER
FAITH	SWORD	BLOOD	BHANGRA	HARVEST	CROPS
DANCING	KACHH	DRUMMERS	COURAGE	KARA

Some Japanese and Chinese festivals

Teacher's Notes

Background information

Kodomo No Hi, or Children's Day, is celebrated in Japan on 5th May each year. It is a day when families celebrate the health, growth and happiness of their children.

This festival is thought to have originated from an ancient Chinese festival and became popular in Japan about fifteen hundred years ago. It is a national holiday and was originally known as Boys' Day. The Japanese also celebrate Hina Matsuri, or Girls' Day, annually on 3rd March but it is not marked as a national holiday, so, due to some feeling that this was unfair, Boys' Day was adapted in 1948 to include both sexes and is now thought of as Children's Day. Despite this, the customs and traditions of Children's Day are still mainly associated with boys.

In Samurai times, armour and helmets were decorated to strengthen the spirit of young boys who were trained and ready to fight from around the age of 15. Today, dolls of famous warriors are displayed in homes and shops on Children's Day. Other customs mainly symbolise strength and success. The koi carp is the symbol of Children's Day as it represents energy, courage and spirit – once thought of as qualities needed for boy warriors, but now recognised as desirable features in all healthy, growing children.

As well as Children's Day and Girls' Day, the Japanese also celebrate a festival called Shichi-Go-San, which means Seven-Five-Three. On this day they celebrate any children aged 7, 5 or 3 as they believe that these are the ages at which children grow the most.

Practical activity

Children could investigate koi carp, their colourings and their characteristics. Use this information to help pupils understand why the characteristics of the carp make them a suitable symbol for Children's Day.

As a number of festivals are covered only briefly here, there is a lot of potential for additional activities to be carried out.

Worksheet 1 Information text on Japanese and Chinese festivals.

Worksheet 2 Template for bamboo flagpole and 'family' koi.

Worksheet 3 Dragon racing boat template. If more than two children are playing you will need to photocopy the counters several times.

Andrew Brodie: Festivals Across the Year 9-11 © A C Black Publishers Ltd. 2007

Some Japanese and Chinese festivals

Read the information below about some Japanese and Chinese festivals.

Japanese Festivals

In May each year, Children's Day is celebrated in Japan. On this day parents are thankful that their children are healthy and growing well. Children are thankful for the love and care given to them by their parents. The festival was called Boys' Day until 1947, because boys used to be thought more important than girls. In 1948 the name was changed to Children's Day.

On Children's Day, flags shaped like fish are flown on bamboo flagpoles outside family homes. The fish are brightly coloured koi carp. There will be one fish flying for each child in the family. Koi carp are used as the symbol of Children's Day, as they are fish that display energy, courage and spirit. People hope that their children might also have these qualities.

In Japan there are also two other festivals about children. In March each year there is a Girls' Day and in November there is a festival called Seven Five Three. The Seven Five Three Festival is for children aged seven, five and three as it was believed that these were the ages when children grew best.

Chinese Festivals

The Lantern Festival occurs on the fifteenth day of the Chinese New Year. It marks the end of the New Year celebrations and lanterns are hung in the streets. People also enjoy watching dragon dancing and fireworks, as well as eating sticky rice dumplings called 'yuanxiao'. The festival dates from ancient times when it was believed that on that night, spirits could be seen by the light of a flaming torch. As time went on, lanterns replaced the torches. These are usually red, as this is the colour of good fortune.

Another Chinese festival that occurs near the beginning of the year is Tomb Sweeping Day. This is a spring festival when people think about their dead ancestors, and go to tidy up their burial places. This is a cheerful festival enjoyed by the whole family. In Chinese tradition, the spirits of the dead ancestors will protect the family in the future, so it is important to keep them happy. This festival also includes the custom of flying kites, and there are often kite flying competitions happening at this time.

The Dragon Boat Festival is another Chinese tradition. The boats used in the races are long narrow rowing boats. They are made to look like very colourful racing dragons in the water. As red is a lucky colour, there can always be some red seen on the boat. In order to keep the crew racing well, there is a drummer on board who beats a steady rhythm to keep them all rowing in time.

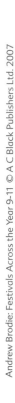

Some Japanese and Chinese festivals

Name .... Date ....

Below you will see a bamboo flagpole and some koi carp of varying sizes. Use these to make the Children's Day flag that would fly outside your home if you were living in Japan.
You may need to read the information on Worksheet 1 to know how many koi carp to use.

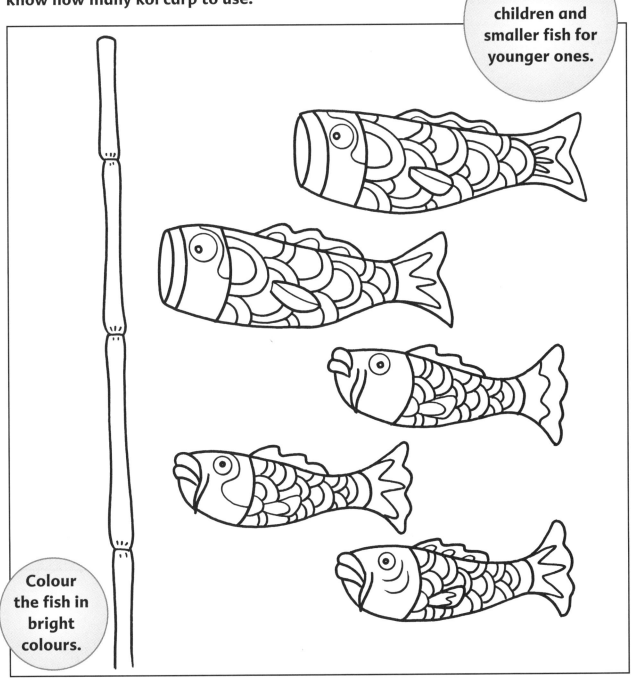

Use larger fish for older children and smaller fish for younger ones.

Colour the fish in bright colours.

Andrew Brodie: Festivals Across the Year 9-11 © A C Black Publishers Ltd. 2007

Stick your finished work into your book and give it a title. Write a sentence or two about Children's Day.

Some Japanese and Chinese festivals

Name ....

Date ....

Design a Dragon Boat Race board game.

On a large sheet of paper, design a Dragon Boat Race board game. You may wish to add instructions on some of the squares, such as 'Stop to watch the kite-flying competition. Miss a turn.'

Use the main outline below as your counter. Carefully colour your boat before folding it, so that it stands upright. You may wish to add some racers and a drummer to your boat.

Make sure everybody understands the rules before you begin to play your game.

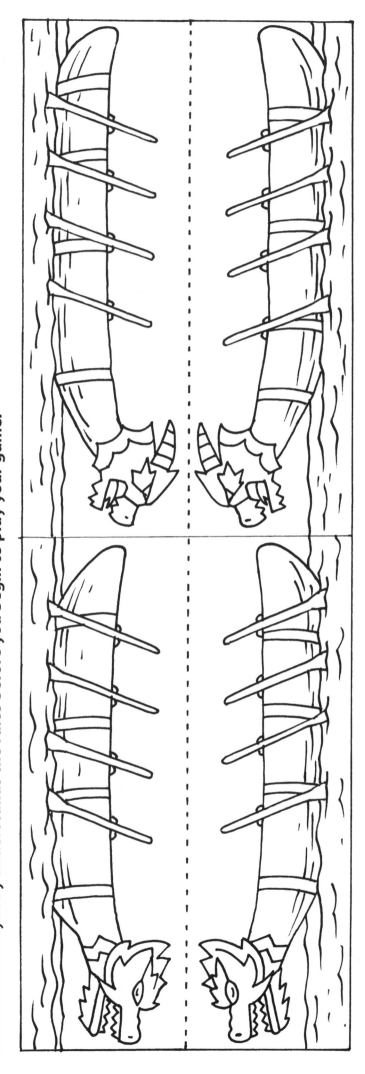

Wesak
Teacher's Notes

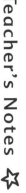

Background information

The festival of Wesak (sometimes spelt Vesak) is the most important in the Buddhist calendar and is celebrated by Buddhists all over the world. Wesak takes place on the day of the full moon in May, or very occasionally in early June. It celebrates the birth, 'Enlightenment' and death of Siddhartha Gautama, who became known as the Buddha, which means 'the Enlightened one'.

Wesak is a very joyful festival, but is generally marked with a day of reflection and holiness, rather than more common festivities such as music and dancing. The Buddha was a holy man who wanted to end suffering and sought happiness and inner peace by rejecting worldly possessions and pleasures. Wesak is a day for all Buddhists to remember the story of the Buddha's 'Enlightenment' by living and promoting the core values of Buddhism which were taught by the Buddha. It is also a time to bring happiness to less fortunate people and money is often donated to charities with this in mind. In Buddhist countries, shops which sell alcohol will often be closed down for two days over Wesak as Buddhists should abstain from alcohol and all other intoxicating substances. Even food is thought of as a human indulgence, and must be eaten in moderation. Any food eaten at Wesak is usually vegetarian, as the Buddha taught that animals should not be harmed.

Buddhists will often clean their houses in preparation for the festival and might help to decorate their local temple with paintings or lights. Buddhists will go to the temple early on the morning of Wesak to meditate and to reaffirm their faith. They may bring small offerings of candles, joss-sticks or flowers (lotus) for the monks to remind them of how all life must eventually come to an end, like that of a flower or candle. It is important to understand that the Buddha is not worshipped as a god, but is thought of as a guide whose teachings should be followed by Buddhists worldwide. He is an inspiration for all Buddhists who seek to achieve 'Enlightenment', a state of mind which transcends suffering and human desire.

Buddhism is followed by people from countries in all parts of the world and its customs have often been influenced by the different cultures that have embraced them. As a result, Wesak celebrations vary from country to country. In China, dragon dancing is sometimes part of the Wesak celebrations and in Indonesia and Sri Lanka decorative lanterns are a feature of the festival.

Worksheet 1 Information for pupils to read.

Worksheet 2 Word search - the message below the word search should read: Wesak is celebrated by Buddhists throughout the world.

Worksheet 3 This contains two different Wesak crosswords so that pupils can use their understanding of the festival to invent the clues. Working in pairs, pupils can draw out the crosswords without the answers in order to let their partners try to solve them using their clues.

Andrew Brodie: Festivals Across the Year 9-11 © A C Black Publishers Ltd. 2007

Wesak

The Buddhist festival of Wesak is a joyful event, considered to be the most important of the year. It is held on the day of the full moon in May. Wesak is a celebration of the birth, 'Enlightenment' and death of the Buddha.

In preparation for Wesak, houses are cleaned and brightly decorated with lights and flowers. Light is a key feature of this celebration and lanterns may be used to decorate the streets. Wesak is celebrated in different ways in different countries. In China, there is dragon dancing, whilst in Japan a custom at Wesak is Bathing the Buddha. Water is poured over statues of the Buddha as a reminder that people should wash evil out of their own minds.

As well as enjoying processions, decorations and firework displays, giving is an important part of this festival. At Wesak, Buddhists remember the poor and often give donations or gifts to charities that help to care for the needy. Cards may also be exchanged between friends. Of course, it is also important that Buddhists visit their temples at festival time. There they will take offerings including flowers, incense and candles, and may also present the monks with gifts.

The Buddha

As Wesak celebrates the birth, 'Enlightenment' and death of the Buddha, it is useful to know a little about him.

The Buddha was born about 2500 years ago. His name was Siddhartha Gautama and as he was the son of a noble family, he lived a privileged life.

When he was a young man, he went outside the palace grounds for the first time and he saw many things that made him realise that life included suffering, sickness and death.

The happiest person he met was a holy man who was very content without large amounts of money or earthly possessions. Gautama began to follow his example. Once he had found the way to true contentment, he wished to be known as the Buddha, which means 'the Enlightened one'.

He spent many years travelling around India teaching people how they should live their lives. Many people now follow his teachings and there are millions of Buddhists in many parts of the world.

Andrew Brodie: Festivals Across the Year 9–11 © A C Black Publishers Ltd. 2007

Wesak

Name .... Date ....

Find the words from the flower in the grid below. Lightly shade each word you find.

INCENSE   LANTERNS   ENLIGHTENMENT
PROCESSION   CARDS   MONKS   GIFTS
WESAK   BIRTH   DEATH   DECORATIONS
TEMPLE   BUDDHA   SIDDHARTHA
FULL MOON

W	A	H	D	D	U	B	E	X	S	K	D	Z
A	S	I	D	D	H	A	R	T	H	A	E	N
J	K	V	E	I	Q	S	X	C	G	S	C	O
E	L	A	N	T	E	R	N	S	I	E	O	I
L	T	E	Z	B	J	B	R	A	F	W	R	S
H	V	T	E	D	M	B	I	Y	T	X	A	S
F	U	L	L	M	O	O	N	R	S	B	T	E
S	E	U	D	D	N	H	C	I	T	S	I	C
D	T	L	S	Q	K	X	E	T	H	H	O	O
R	R	O	P	Z	S	U	N	G	J	H	N	R
A	V	O	V	M	U	X	S	T	T	H	S	P
C	E	J	W	O	E	R	E	V	Q	L	X	D
E	N	L	I	G	H	T	E	N	M	E	N	T

Now shade the remaining letters X Z J V Q.

Starting at the top and reading from left to right, the unshaded letters should spell out a message. Find the message and write it in the space below.

— — — — — —   — —   — — — — — — — —

— —   — — — — — — — — —

— — — — — — — — —   — — —

— — — — — .

Andrew Brodie: Festivals Across the Year 9-11 © A C Black Publishers Ltd. 2007

Wesak

Name .... Date ....

Crossword One

Look at the completed crossword below. No clues have been written for it. Write clues for the crosswords, copy the grid onto squared paper and give it to your partner to complete.

```
                          ¹W
²F      ³B             E
E      U      ⁴M       S
⁵S  I  D  D  H  A  R  T  H  A
T      D      Y       A
I      H              K
V      A   ⁶T  E  M  P  L  E
A                  O
⁸L  A  N  T  E  R  N  S
                   K
                   S
```

1 _____

2 _____

3 _____

4 _____

5 _____

6 _____

7 _____

8 _____

Crossword Two

Look at the completed crossword below. No clues have been written for it. Write clues for the crosswords, copy the grid onto squared paper, and give it to your partner to complete.

1 _____

2 _____

```
¹G  A  U  T  A  M  A  ²
I              I
³F  U  L  L  ⁴M  O  O  N
T      L       D
S      I   ⁵B  I  R  T  H⁶
       G       A      O
       H              L
       T              Y
⁷B  U  D  D  H  I  S  T
```

3 _____

4 _____

5 _____

6 _____

7 _____

Andrew Brodie: Festivals Across the Year 9–11 © A C Black Publishers Ltd. 2007

Resource Sheet A: Cycle of festivals

The wheels below show the order in which some of the main festivals occur in each major religion and in the Chinese culture. Each wheel shows more festivals than those featured in this book. This enables the information to be used when studying a particular religion. The exact dates of many of these festivals vary from year to year.

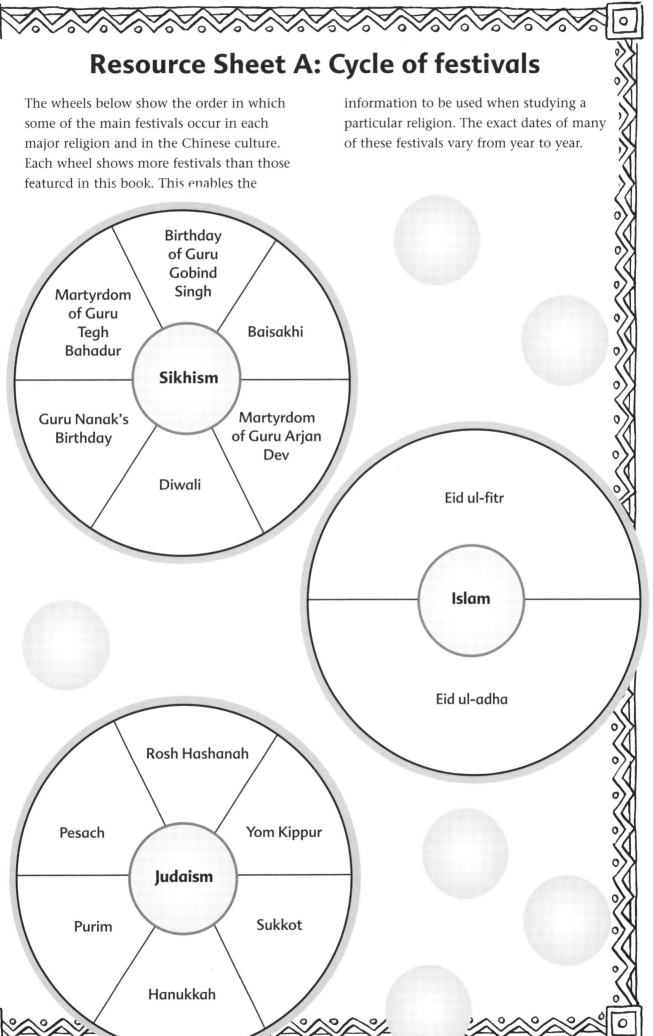

Sikhism wheel:
- Birthday of Guru Gobind Singh
- Baisakhi
- Martyrdom of Guru Arjan Dev
- Diwali
- Guru Nanak's Birthday
- Martyrdom of Guru Tegh Bahadur

Islam wheel:
- Eid ul-fitr
- Eid ul-adha

Judaism wheel:
- Rosh Hashanah
- Yom Kippur
- Sukkot
- Hanukkah
- Purim
- Pesach

Andrew Brodie: Festivals Across the Year 9–11 © A C Black Publishers Ltd 2007

Resource Sheet B: Cycle of festivals

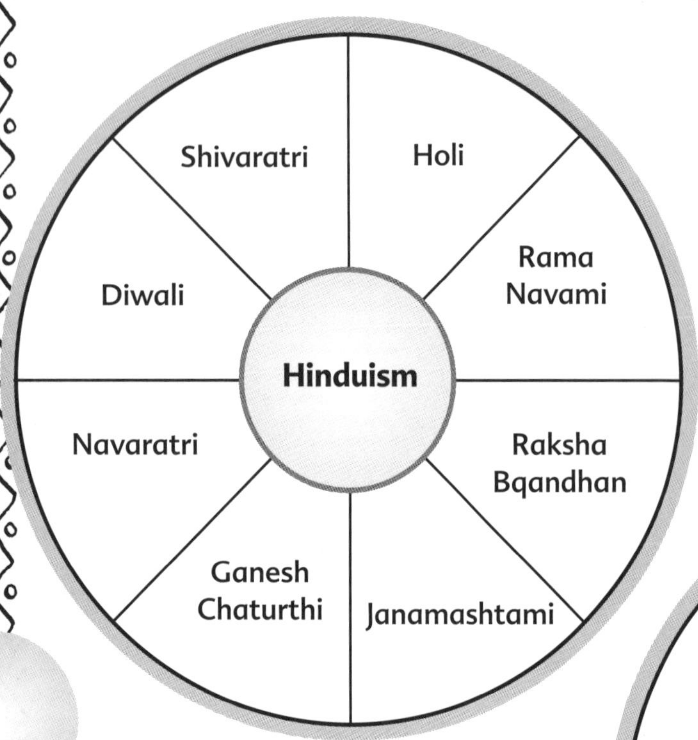

Hinduism
- Shivaratri
- Holi
- Rama Navami
- Raksha Bqandhan
- Janamashtami
- Ganesh Chaturthi
- Navaratri
- Diwali

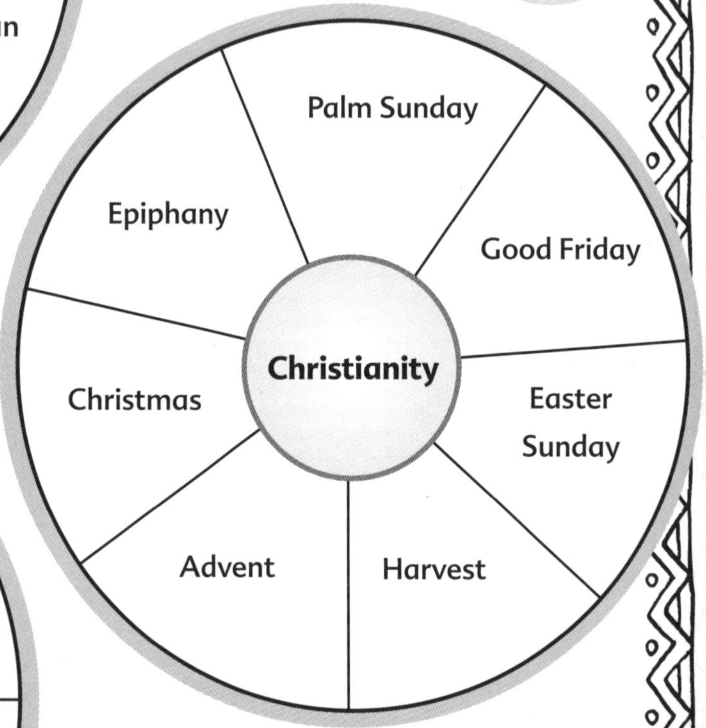

Christianity
- Palm Sunday
- Good Friday
- Easter Sunday
- Harvest
- Advent
- Christmas
- Epiphany

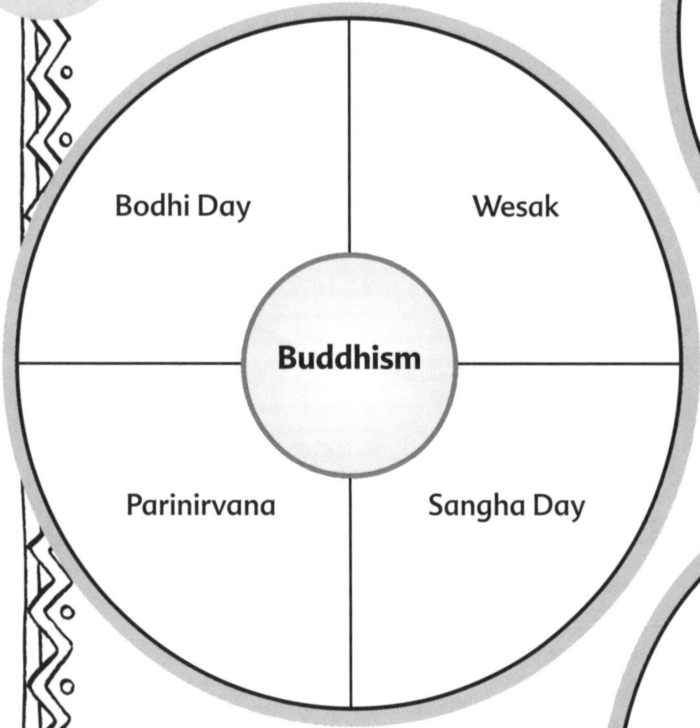

Buddhism
- Bodhi Day
- Wesak
- Sangha Day
- Parinirvana

Chinese Culture
- Dragon Boat Festival
- Chinese New Year
- Lantern Festival
- Ching Ming

Andrew Brodie: Festivals Across the Year 9–11 © A C Black Publishers Ltd. 2007

Resource Sheet C: Religious Symbols

Sikhism

Islam

Hinduism

Andrew Brodie: Festivals Across the Year 9-11 © A C Black Publishers Ltd. 2007

Resource Sheet D: Religious Symbols

Buddhism

Christianity

Judaism

Resource Sheet E

Festivals Word Puzzle

The puzzle below contains words that all have a connection to the festivals you have studied. To find out what the words are you must work out what letter is represented by each number. Some of the letters have been provided to start you off . As you find each new letter enter it into the grid at the bottom of the page, and cross it off the list down the side of the page. Good luck.

1	2	3	4	5	6	7								
2						8	5	6	7	10	4	2	9	
11	5	12	20	5	2	3								
15								16	2	3	14	6		
13	5	6		6	10	13	1				5			
13				7		10				16				
2			14	3	2	21	17	11	16		17			
1	17	9	10	3			14	1		3				
		12				15		3		2				
	5	2	6	7	5	3	9	10	21	1	7	6		
		9					6		10					
18	2	10	6	2	13	1	10	7		17				
			2				10		11					
			3				2		6					
16	5	9	5	18	3	2	7	10	17	11				

Alphabet list (right side): A B C D E F G H I J K L M N O P Q R S T U V W X Y Z

1 H	2 A	3 R	4	5	6	7	8	9	10	11	12	13
14	15	16	17	18	19 Z	20	21	22 J	23 X	24 Q	25 P	26 M

The nineteen words in the grid are just some of the forty printed below.

ANGEL	DRAGON	KES	RELIGION
BUDDHIST	EASTER	KIRPAN	RAMA
BAISAKHI	FESTIVAL	LAKSHMI	SIKH
BETHLEHEM	FUN	LIGHTS	SITA
CARDS	HANUKKAH	MOSQUE	STAR
CELEBRATIONS	HARVEST	NEW YEAR	SUKKOT
CHRISTMAS	HINDU	PEACE	WESAK
COLOUR	HOLI	PESACH	
DANCING	JEWISH	PROSPERITY	
DECORATIONS	KARA	RANGOLI	

Resource Sheet F

Festivals Crossword

Solve the clues to correctly fill the word puzzle grid below.

Clues Across

1. The religion that celebrates Guru Nanak's Birthday
2. The Rama and Sita story is enjoyed by members of this faith
5. The spring festival that celebrates the death and resurrection of Jesus Christ
6. A Christian festival celebrated on 25th December
8. Jewish festival of light
10. Sikh festival usually taking place on 13th April
11. A Hindu spring festival that can include throwing coloured powders over one another

Clues Down

1. Jewish festival that includes building huts that may be lived in for one week
3. A Buddhist festival held on the day of the full moon in May.
4. The Jewish Passover festival
7. The month in which healthy Muslim adults fast from dawn until dusk each day
9. Hindu festival of lights